STUDY SKILLS
STRATEGIES

STUDY SKILLS STRATEGIES
How to Learn More in Less Time

Uelaine Lengefeld

KOGAN PAGE

Copyright © Crisp Publications Inc 1987

First published in the United States of America
in 1987 by Crisp Publications Inc, 95 First Street,
Los Altos, California 94022, USA.

This edition first published in Great Britain in
1988 by Kogan Page Ltd, 120 Pentonville Road,
London N1 9JN

British Library Cataloguing in Publication Data

Lengefeld, Uelaine
  Study skills strategies.
  1. Study techniques – Manuals
  I. Title
  371.3′028′12

  ISBN 1-85091-738-8
  ISBN 1-85091-737-X Pbk

Printed and bound in Great Britain by
Biddles Ltd, Guildford, Surrey

Contents

Acknowledgements

Special thanks go to Elwood Chapman for his ideas and for his special mentoring throughout the creation of this book. Without Mr Chapman and the assistance of Tonie Lauren, who typed the material and added her graphics talent, the first edition would never have come to fruition.

I am especially grateful to Marcie Skinner and Leticia Guzman for their endless revisions of the manuscript, and to Joann Henderson, research assistant, for her background in cognitive psychology.

My students and tutors in the Educational Opportunity Program deserve special thanks for helping to suggest exercises. The materials used in tutor training, classes and workshops were supported by Jim Lopez and Moses Walters, EOP Director and Associate Director. I appreciate their confidence in me and this project.

I also want to acknowledge Professors Walter Pauk, Lilian Metlitzky, Martha Maxwell, and Frank Robinson for research contributions in the field of learning and reading skills.

Michael Crisp's talented editorial pen, and belief in the book have been essential. I am grateful for his valuable assistance.

Finally, and most importantly, this book is dedicated to Katherine Lengefeld, my daughter, because she uses these study skills strategies and because she has always believed in me and my dreams.

To the Reader

Fear of the unknown is both normal and healthy. It can be a powerful motivator. On the other hand, too much fear can cause procrastination, and in some cases, paralysis. If you learn proven study skills strategies much of the fear about school or college (or any new learning experience), will fade.

Your anxiety will diminish and your confidence will grow once you are familiar with the *study* skills in this book that were designed to help you accomplish the following objectives:

1. Learning to analyse your attitudes towards studying, and your current study skills habits.
2. Making a commitment to practise new study skills strategies.
3. Achieving a sense of personal power, thanks to the time management and goal setting exercises you will complete.
4. Taking clear, meaningful class notes and learning how to study from them.
5. Developing power reading skills such as SQ3R which will teach you to systematically mark and take study notes on a college level textbook.
6. Acquiring better methods to memorise material for long-term recall.
7. Developing organisational patterns which will help you use imagery to visualise concepts and encode new material.
8. Learning how to prepare for, and take, objective exams.
9. Understanding the techniques which will assist you to write better essays.
10. Using study aids and oral recitation which can improve your performance on tests.

All these objectives can be achieved. It will take effort on your part, but if you are serious about your studies, will be well worth the time you invest.

Uelaine A Lengefeld

Preface

A vast majority of students do not learn effective study skills. As a result, they never achieve their potential in an academic programme. *Study Skills Strategies* is a refreshing, time-saving, and inexpensive method to acquire quality study skills.

The learning strategies in this module are flexible. For example, this book can easily be integrated into summer or weekend college preparatory sessions, or used effectively in workshops for re-entry students.

When a student reaches out for help, a comprehensive, theoretical book is overwhelming. Thanks to the brevity and readability of this manual, students react positively. Even without a formal class, students can make progress, thanks to the self-study format.

We have made every effort to keep *Study Skills Strategies* simple and practical so readers will keep it as a quick reference to refresh themselves as the need arises.

1. Getting Started: Your Attitude Towards Studying

This section of *Study Skills Strategies* was designed to help you to know yourself better. The exercises and self-assessments are for your personal information. There are no right answers – but for this programme to be effective, you must be honest with yourself.

Throughout the book you will find boxes called 'Learning Trampolines'. These will help you to practise and apply some of the more important concepts that have been presented.

Discover your attitude towards studying

To learn and apply quality study skills, it is essential to have a positive attitude. In fact, your attitude and motivation will make all the difference. To measure your attitude towards studying, complete this exercise. If the statement describes your attitude or study habit tick 'Yes' and if not tick 'No'. *Be very honest.*

Attitudes	Yes	No
1. I am satisfied with my test scores on most examinations.	☐	☐
2. If I do poorly in a test, I increase my efforts and get help from a teacher, a tutor, or a study partner.	☐	☐
3. When required, I can concentrate on studying. I am not easily distracted.	☐	☐

4. The challenge of taking study notes on a difficult textbook reading does not throw me. ☐ ☐

5. Although I am busy I can still find priority time to study. Procrastination and cramming are not problems for me. ☐ ☐

6. I attend class regularly and carefully prepare for most class sessions. ☐ ☐

7. I have a clear reason for going to school and know that good study skills will get me closer to my career goal. ☐ ☐

8. When I have a boring teacher, I realise I must work harder to make the material interesting. ☐ ☐

9. My moods or personal problems seldom prevent me from completing my work. ☐ ☐

10. I can visualise myself passing the exams. ☐ ☐

11. I know how to reward myself for finishing a difficult assignment. ☐ ☐

12. I listen carefully while taking class notes, and I revise them within 24 hours. ☐ ☐

For any item where you ticked No, be sure to read carefully the section of this book devoted to that particular study skill. This book has helped hundreds of students, and it can help you.

Many students fail a course or drop out because they have not learned how to study. The facing page contains some typical comments from whose who succeed, and those who do not. Which best describes you?

Make your choice now!

Place a tick by those comments that may sound like you.

Survivor comments

— I can hang on until the work is done.

— I have chosen a career direction and am excited about my choice.

— I am not afraid to ask for help when I need it.

— I can concentrate when required.

— My textbook is read and marked before each class, and I revise my class notes each day.

— My time management is getting better all the time.

— I can visualise myself passing the exams.

Drop-out comments

— I studied for the test, and still failed! I give up! What's the use?

— I'm bored, and might cut class today. I don't know why I am taking this class anyway.

— I don't need help from a tutor.

— My mind wanders; I just can't concentrate. Where does the time go?

— I read the textbook over and over, but I can't remember anything I read.

— I'm so sleepy; I'll cram later.

— No one cares if I pass.

After reviewing your choices, place an X in the boxes that best describe your attitude.

1. ☐ I want to be a survivor, but doubt I'll succeed.

2. ☐ It would be nice to succeed; maybe I'll try a few of the ideas in this book.

3. ☐ I want to learn academic skills that will help me to excel, not just 'survive'.

2. Time Control

Learning to say 'No' to the voice inside your head that says 'I'm too tired to study,' or 'Let's go to a party' is absolutely necessary for academic success. This does not mean school must be a boring grind – it simply means that you must learn to control your time to ensure there is room for both serious study *and* enjoyment.

The following pages provide several time control tips, techniques and strategies. By following the ten Time Control Tips presented, you will be able to design your own flexible study timetable.

It is a good idea to follow carefully the timetable you complete for two or three weeks (making minor adjustments as needed) until it becomes routine. Remember there are such things as 'good habits' too!

Time control questions and tips

	Tick when completed	Date
1. **Do you have a large monthly calendar?** Write all important tests, deadlines, and activities on a large monthly calendar. Place it in a conspicuous place. Use colour to highlight important dates – red dots or red pen.	☐	_____

	Tick when completed	Date

2. Do you have a weekly appointment calendar?
Purchase one that shows a 'week-at-a-glance' so you have a good view of the entire week.

☐ _____

3. Do you have a weekly study plan?
Use the blank weekly study plan on page 23 to visualise and organise your time. Lightly pencil your classes in (by title on the days and times they meet) and block in times to eat, sleep, work, or study. Use this code (or one like it):

☐ _____

E = Exercise	**J** = Job
S = Study	**X** = Free Time
C = Commute	**Z** = Sleep

4. Do you plan for at least one hour of study for each class period?
Protect time each day for study. By keeping a regular timetable, your study time will soon become habit forming.

☐ _____

5. Do you plan for study breaks?
Remember to limit your straight study time to no longer than one hour. It is important to take a ten-minute break between study periods to refresh yourself, and give your mind a rest.

☐ _____

Tick when Date
completed

6. **Do you preview test assignments and revise classroom notes from the previous class before your study time?**
Build this encoding strategy into your weekly timetable with **P** for preview and **R** for revise. Add these items to your timetable.

☐ ————

7. **Do you make effective use of any commuting time to school each day?**
If you travel to school or college and have an opportunity to do some schoolwork, this is an ideal time to preview or revise. Place a **C** for all commuting time on your timetable.

☐ ————

8. **Do you leave sufficient time for relaxation and play?**
Play is therapeutic. Without it you are only half a person. Make sure you have plenty of play time (marked with a **P**) on your calendar. Meditation is a relaxing way to begin or end your busy day.

☐ ————

9. **Do you reward yourself for meeting goals?**
No matter how tight your budget, you can always afford a date, a film, an ice cream (or anything else that motivates you). Do not accept your 'reward' if you do not meet your goal!

☐ ————

**Tick when Date
completed**

10. Are you a list maker? ☐ _____
It's a great idea to keep lists. Assign a
priority to items on your list and try
to complete the most important ones
first. Carry forward items not completed on your next day's/week's
list.

Learning Trampoline
List five (5) things you have to do before tomorrow. Top priority
items are A; next in priority are B; less urgent are C.

A, B, or C   **Mini-priority list**

_____   1._____

_____   2._____

_____   3._____

_____   4._____

_____   5._____

Now label each item as an A, B, or C priority. Complete the As first!

Exercise: 1. When do you plan for the next day or week?_____

2. When do you revise your notes from the
previous week?_____

3. How many times a week do you revise the text or
notes for a class?_____

Sample weekly study timetable

	MON	TUE	WED	THU	FRI	SAT	SUN
6–7			BREAKFAST			WORK	
7–8		GET READY FOR SCHOOL					
8–9	HIST.	CHEM.	HIST.	CHEM.	HIST		
9–10	STUDY		STUDY		STUDY		
10–11		STUDY		STUDY			CHURCH
11–12	FRENCH		FRENCH		FRENCH		
12–1			LUNCH				
1–2	MATHS	WORK	MATHS	STUDY	MATHS	WORK	STUDY
2–3	STUDY		STUDY	CHEM.	STUDY		
3–4				LAB.			
4–5	ENG.		ENG.		ENG.		
5–6	STUDY		STUDY	STUDY	STUDY		
6–7			DINNER				
7–8	STUDY	STUDY	STUDY	STUDY			STUDY
8–9							
9–10							
10–11							

Begin making lists today. Copy this page and use it as a model for a week, then adapt your own form. List making should become a habit.

Today's priority list

Date: _____

Priority A, B, or C	School	Done
_____	1. _____	[ ]
_____	2. _____	[ ]
_____	3. _____	[ ]
_____	4. _____	[ ]
_____	5. _____	[ ]
_____	6. _____	[ ]
_____	7. _____	[ ]
_____	8. _____	[ ]
_____	9. _____	[ ]
_____	10. _____	[ ]
	Personal	
_____	1. _____	[ ]
_____	2. _____	[ ]
_____	3. _____	[ ]
_____	4. _____	[ ]
_____	5. _____	[ ]
_____	6. _____	[ ]
_____	7. _____	[ ]

Suggestions. Be realistic. Plan to accomplish a few projects or errands each day. As you complete an item, tick it. You may need to lower your expectations and increase your performance. (Make copies for each day.)

STOP! This blank weekly study timetable should be filled in in pencil at first. Your final timetable will probably not be completed until you have completed this programme. Look at the sample on page 21 for guidance.

	MON	TUE	WED	THU	FRI	SAT	SUN
6–7							
7–8							
8–9							
9–10							
10–11							
11–12							
12–1							
1–2							
2–3							
3–4							
4–5							
5–6							
6–7							
7–8							
8–9							
9–10							
10–11							

3. Notetaking Techniques

Important notetaking techniques

1. Always read your assignment before you come to class. Otherwise, the lecture may make little sense. **Be prepared!**
2. Find a seat near the front of the room. Up close, you can see the board, be more aware of facial expressions, hear better, and not daydream or snooze as easily.
3. Identify some 'serious' students in each class and get to know them. Get phone numbers in case you have questions or need help during the term.
4. Copy everything the teacher writes on the board. This is especially true of examples, solutions, outlines, and definitions.
5. Organise and index your notes with coloured tabs. If notes are allowed in any exam, you'll be ahead of the game.

Warning!
Do not try to write down every word the teacher says. Listen for the main ideas. Abbreviate, omit, and invent.

Learning Trampoline

As soon as possible get a phone number from a student in each of your classes. Your instructor can make this easier by asking who is willing to participate in a telephone exchange and then providing a master list of numbers.

Class	Name	Phone number

Effective listening: the secret of better class notes

An outline format has been used below to refresh your memory on outlining skills.

1. **Get organised**
   A. Use a spiral or 3-hole notebook to keep your notes organised. Avoid loose-leaf folders that allow your papers to flutter everywhere. Yellow paper may be easier on your eyes, so consider changing from white to yellow.
   B. Date each lecture and number all pages for that course in sequence.

2. **Set up your format**
   A. Study the sample format on page 28. Use it, or experiment with something similar until you have a format you like.

   B. Recall words or cues to main ideas should be written in the left margin of the right-hand page. Fill in recall words when you first revise your notes. Study questions should be written on the facing left-hand page to assist you when you revise.

   C. In your own words, summarise the main ideas at the bottom of the right-hand page (or write questions you need to ask your instructor).

   D. Use an outline similar to the one on this page rather than writing full paragraphs.

       1. Indent secondary ideas, supporting document-ation, or examples.

       2. Always leave room when a new point is being developed.

       3. Incomplete sentences or phrases will be necessary (notice phrases used on the sample). Make sure you know the meaning of all your incomplete sentences.

3. **Taking lecture notes**
   A. What should you take notes on?
      1. All definitions
      2. Lists
      3. Formulas or solutions
   B. Indenting is important to set off secondary ideas. Leave plenty of space so the notes are easier to study.
   C. Draw arrows to show connections between ideas.
   D. Whenever you are in doubt, *write it down*. In discussion classes, jot notes on important points – particularly conclusions reached during the discussion.
   E. Spell new words as well as you can by the sound. Look up correct spelling the first chance you get, or ask your instructor for help.
   F. Use symbols, diagrams, or drawings to simplify ideas.

4. **Listening**
   A. Listen for the following signals from your instructor about what is important:
      - Voice changes usually indicate important points – listen for increases in volume or dramatic pauses.
      - Repetition is a clue that an important point is being made.
      - Gestures may indicate a major point.
   B. Stay involved in all classroom discussions. Ask questions, especially when things are becoming unclear.

5. **Participate in class**
   A. Think, react, reflect, and question to help your teacher to keep the class alive.
   B. Become involved but don't be a clown. Do not dominate the conversation.
   C. Your marks will often improve if you participate actively. If you are on the borderline between grades, most teachers will remember your desire to learn if you participate.

Sample notes

Use the recall cues on the 'Classroom Notes' side to answer the study questions on the facing page. Write your answers on the lines provided.

STUDY NOTES & QUESTIONS OR TEXTBOOK NOTES		CLASSROOM NOTES MEMORISING STRATEGIES	
			9/7/88
	Recall		
	Cues		
What are 2 types of memory:	MEM?	I. Memory – types of	
[1]	LT	A. Long term	
[2]	ST	B. Short term	
What are 3 memory tips:	GIM?	C. Strategies	
[1]	Mneu	1. Mnemonics	
[2]	S. Sent	2. Silly Sentences	
[3]	Vis	3. Visualisation	
	Use this space for:		
	1. Summary in your own words, or		
	2. Questions, or		
	3. New vocabulary		

Compare your answers with those of the author at the bottom of the page.

Answers: 1. Long term   2. Short term
1. Mnemonics   2. Silly sentences
3. Visualisation

Improve your notetaking

Speed writing can be increased by simplifying your handwriting.

• Practise writing a sentence in your normal handwriting in the space below.

_____

_____

• Observe these inefficient notes with excessive loops. Now look at your sample (above) does it have any excessive loops? Notice how difficult they are to decipher.

Note taking is not the time for fancy writing

• Simplify your handwriting; some printing may be necessary.

Note taking is the time to simplify. Change I to I.

Revise immediately

Whenever possible, *spend 5–20 minutes* revising your notes immediately after class. Fill in missing areas and rewrite garbled notes. Studies show that short periods of study improve long-term memory.

A tape recorder can be an asset but do not use it as a crutch or substitute for taking notes!

Use abbreviations

ABBREVIATE, OMIT, INVENT
AND SIMPLIFY

Commonly used abbreviations:

>	increase	=	equals
<	decrease	ex	example
∴	therefore	def	definition
∵	because	ie	that is
➜	caused, led to	v	versus
w/	with	≡	identical to
≠	unequal	imp	important
w/o	without	sig	significant
⊙	individual		

Omit vowels

mn = main   unnec = unnecessary
bkgd = background

Invent your own abbreviations common to your discipline:

subc	= subconscious	△	= change
sftwr	= software	△'ed	= changed
exst	= existential	△ing	= changing
ct	= computer terminal	△'able	= changeable
chrm	= chromosomes		

Do you use other abbreviations? Add your own below:

_____

_____

_____

_____

_____

Learning Trampoline

Homework

1. Take notes on a class lecture. Indent, use phrases, and revise your notes by placing recall cues in the left hand margin.

2. After taking your notes, highlight the main points. Next, ask your instructor to evaluate the quality of the notes you took and make suggestions.

3. If you are working with a tutor bring your notes to each meeting.

4. Critical Reading Skills

Effective reading is probably the most important element of becoming a quality student.

Unfortunately, not everyone is blessed with good reading ability. Like any other skill, however, reading can be developed and improved with practice.

In the pages ahead, you will be introduced to a five-step reading strategy that will help to improve your reading skills by becoming a more critical reader.

This strategy is called SQ3R.

SQ3R for success

When you read a love letter, you savour each word and have absolutely no difficulty concentrating. You do not need to underline the main ideas or make marginal notes. Textbook reading is different. You must learn to apply special reading and marking skills when you study complicated materials. An expansion of the SQ3R reading technique (explained below) can reduce your study time and significantly increase your ability grasp essential information.

Do you know the SQ3R technique?
Read carefully the five steps involved in SQ3R and then apply them to the sample textbook selection.

Overview of SQ3R

STEP 1:   SURVEY

STEP 2:   QUESTION

STEP 3:   READ AND UNDERLINE

STEP 4:   RECITE AND WRITE

STEP 5:   REVIEW

Step 1. Survey

Spend no more than *10 minutes* to take a 'sneak preview' of the reading you have been assigned. You may not be in the habit of previewing and will have to force this important first step consciously. Previewing provides an overview of the way the chapter is organised. Smart travellers use a road map, and smart students survey first. You should:

- **Examine the title of each chapter.**
- **Note headings and subheadings and the relationship between the important headings in each chapter.**
- **Glance at diagrams, graphs or visuals.**
- **Quickly skim the introductory and concluding sections of each chapter.**
- **Notice any study questions or activities at the end of the chapter.**

Step 2. Question

Begin with the first section of a chapter. Always read with the intent to answer a question. By using the words **who, what, when, where,** or **how,** turn each heading into a question.

See if you can do this by writing two questions for Step 1 and Step 2:
(Check below for the author's answer.)

1. _____
2. _____

Step 3. Read and underline

Read each section with the question you developed in mind. *After* reading the section, go back to the beginning and *underline, highlight, and/or mark the material* using the techniques covered in this book.

Speed reading techniques should not be used for technical material because important details may be missed. Do not be afraid to move your lips or read aloud. Critical reading may require you to reread items several times to understand a sentence or passage completely.

Use a ball point pen to mark your text because pencil fades. Purchase a highlighter to emphasise important information.

A. Underline after reading

Read a paragraph or a section of the text and then *go back and underline only the main points.* <u>Do not underline the first time you read the material.</u>

B. Use numbers for the following:

Use numbers for: 1. lists
2. enumerations, or
3. sequences.

C. Vertical lines

Place vertical lines in the margin to emphasise main points of several lines.

D. Asterisks*

* Use asterisks for main points and for other important points or ideas that may be important.

---

1. 'Why is surveying important?' or 'How do I survey a chapter?'
2. 'How do I create questions from the heading of a section?'

E. Recall phrases
Place recall phrases in the margin to condense major points and provide supporting details. Summaries and questions may also be placed in the margin.

F. Definitions and examples
Underline all definitions. Write 'def' in the margin. Put ( ) parentheses around examples. If you underline or highlight the entire example, your page will be a mass of yellow and your purpose for marking will be lost.

G. Circles or boxes
Some students like to (circle) important concepts, ideas or subheadings.

Other students prefer a box .

H. Highlighting
Highlight the points underlined or highlight in place of underlining. Use a felt tip pen. Yellow is often preferred.

J. ??!!
React to what you read. Agree, disagree, question!
Stay involved with the ideas in the text!

K. Practice
As with any skill, practice is the best way to learn. Would you be confident that you could drive a car after simply listening to a lecture? Show your instructor a sample of your 'markings' until you are confident you are selecting the most important material in each paragraph.

Learning Trampoline
You try it!
Read the paragraphs on the facing page, and then underline or highlight and add recall phrases in the left margin. To save time, underline and mark *only the second paragraph*.

Read, underline and make marginal notations

READ WITH A QUESTION IN MIND. ➤ *Should we leave the Common Market*

It would be a mistake to leave the Common Market. If we did so, it would be because of short-term problems such as agriculture and fishing. These can be solved in time, along with others such as our monetary contribution and EEC restrictive practices. In time these problems will recede, and we shall be more conscious of truly substantial long-term economic and political gains.

LOOK FOR THE TOPIC SENTENCES. ➤

COLUMN FOR MARGINAL NOTATIONS (RECALL CUES)

Much of the negative publicity about the Common Market is about cows and fish. France, as an initial and powerful member of the EC, established for herself and for European agriculture a system of subsidy under which, for example, each cow is financially supported to the sum of £100. Overproduction for guaranteed high prices causes 'butter mountains', which are sold at reduced rates outside the EC, to the understandable anger of British people. But it is unlikely that a system so contrary to common sense will persist over time, although, inconsistently, we seek similar protection (though to a lesser extent) for our fishermen, who argue for a 12-mile limit to keep out Continental fishermen, who could soon turn parts of Devon and Cornwall into deserted villages. Fishing, as a more recent problem than agriculture, is likely to be more quickly solved, but the problem of agriculture will not deny resolution.

Other problems, too, edge their way towards solution. We do not argue that we, as a country, should recoup in benefits the last penny of our annual financial contribution, but a return of £1 back for every £2 in is a situation with which our European partners sympathise. Nor are we happy when West Germany keeps out British lawnmowers on the pretence of their noise, though again inconsistently, we are not beyond keeping out foreign turkeys at Christmas on 'health' grounds. However, the Commission is currently working to harmonise rules and regulations, and this problem is likely to be short-lived.

More deep-rooted are the benefits and opportunities offered by EC membership in economic terms. Movement between the countries of the EC is already much easier, and EC work permits can be obtained. A number of British motorists have benefited by some £1,500 in buying cars on the Continent, and from our

37

industry's point of view, absence of tariffs makes Europe our market. The arrangement offers us an opportunity not a gift: our products must be substantial and at the right price. But this is an opportunity that British workmanship and the British worker are well able to take.

In world political terms, Britain has lost an Empire and not yet quite found a new soul. Though a late and somewhat reluctant member of the EC, our future political identity lies within it. We may regret the passing of pounds, shillings and pence, but the EC is for a 'United States of Europe' with nationalities intact, not for a 'Uniform Europe' with nationalities diminished. Already the ideal of a united Europe has found expression in reality: Europe supported Britain over the Falklands. We can have a new world role no less important than our last one, as part of a third world power block to lend stability to the balance of the superpowers.

It would be a backward step without parallel to leave the Common Market. Budget bills, butter mountains and fishing limits seem large issues now, but they will have been forgotten among the economic and political benefits of the next century.

Reprinted with the permission of the author. Howard Barlow: *How to Succeed in A Levels*. London: Kogan Page.

Compare your underlining and marginal notations with the author's example below

No, we shouldn't leave the Common Market.

It would be a <u>mistake</u> to leave the Common Market. If we did so, it would be because of short-term <u>problems</u> such as agriculture and fishing. These <u>can be solved</u> in time, along with others such as our monetary contribution and EEC restrictive practices. In time these problems will recede, and we shall be more conscious of truly substantial long-term economic and political gains.

Problems:
1. Cows and agriculture.

<u>Much of the negative publicity about the Common Market is about cows and fish</u>. France, as an initial and powerful member of the EC, established for herself and for European agriculture a system of subsidy under which, for example, each <u>cow</u> is financially supported to the sum of £100. Overproduction for guaranteed high prices causes 'butter mountains', which are sold at reduced rates outside the EC, to the understandable

2. Fish.

anger of British people. But it is unlikely that a system so contrary to common sense will persist over time, although, inconsistently, we seek similar protection (though to a lesser extent) for our <u>fishermen</u>, who argue for a 12-mile limit to keep out Continental fishermen, who could soon turn parts of Devon and Cornwall into deserted villages. Fishing, as a more recent problem than agriculture, is likely to be more quickly solved, but the problem of agriculture will not deny resolution.

3. Money contribution.

<u>Other problems</u>, too, edge their way towards solution. We do not argue that we, as a country, should recoup in benefits the last penny of our annual <u>financial contribution</u>, but a return of £1 back for every £2 in is a situation with which our European partners sympathise. Nor are we happy when West Germany keeps out British lawnmowers on the pretence of their noise, though again inconsistently, we are not beyond keeping out foreign turkeys at Christmas on 'health' grounds. However, the Commission is currently working to harmonise rules and regulations, and this problem is likely to be short-lived.

Benefits:
1. Movement.
2. Trade and industry.

<u>More deep-rooted are the benefits and opportunities offered by EC membership in economic terms.</u> <u>Movement</u> between the countries of the EC is already much easier, and EC work permits can be obtained. A number of British motorists have benefited by some £1,500 in buying cars on the Continent, and from our <u>industry's</u> point of view, absence of tariffs makes Europe our <u>market</u>. The arrangement offers us an opportunity not a gift: our products must be substantial and at the right price. But this is an opportunity that British workmanship and the British worker are well able to take.

3. Political.
A new world role.

<u>In world political terms, Britain has lost an Empire and not yet quite found a new soul.</u> Though a late and somewhat reluctant member of the EC, our future political identity lies within it. We may regret the passing of pounds, shillings and pence, but the EC is for a 'United States of Europe' with nationalities intact, not for a 'Uniform Europe' with nationalities diminished. Already the ideal of a united Europe has found expression in reality: Europe supported Britain over the Falklands. We can have <u>a new world role</u> no less important than our last one, <u>as part of a third world power block</u> to lend stability to the balance of the superpowers.

Conclusion:	It would be a <u>backward step</u> without parallel to leave
A backward step	the Common Market. Budget bills, butter mountains
to leave the	and fishing limits seem large issues now, <u>but they will</u>
Common Market.	<u>have been forgotten</u> among the economic and political
The problems will	benefits of the next century.
disappear.	

Step 4. Recite and write study notes and/or recall cues in the margins

Once you have formed questions on your reading and have read to answer those questions, you are ready to recite the answers. Use your underlining and markings to guide you. *Recite the answers out loud (or to yourself).* Also *write brief study notes* which will help to encode the information in your long-term memory for easier retrieval on the final examination.

Write a sentence summary of the main idea in each paragraph if the material is extremely difficult for you.

The recall cues you wrote in the margins are an essential step. If you use those cues to recite, you may not need study notes in some classes.

Step 5. Revise the entire chapter

Once you have read an entire chapter, section by section, you are ready to revise.

This is the *final* step in understanding the material.

1. *Reread* each main heading.
2. *Revise* the underlined and highlighted material.
3. *Answer* the questions you formed for each section. Use your reading notes to help you review.

Learning Trampoline

After you finish steps 3, 4 and 5, select a chapter in one of your texctbooks and mark, highlight, and make brief study notes (1 to 1½ pages only). Then ask your instructor (or tutor) to review your notes with the underlining and recall cues in the margins, and have that person make suggestions for improvement.

---

5. Memory Training

Human beings are capable of extraordinary feats of memory. Even the 'memory experts' agree that their skill was not all due to an inborn ability, but was developed through the use of various techniques, and considerable practice.

Like the experts, you too can improve your memory. In the next few pages, several steps will be presented which, if learned and practised, can make your studying not only easier but more rewarding.

Steps for memory training

Have you studied for hours trying to memorise material for a test and then gone 'blank'? To help you reduce 'blanking out', practise the following memory strategies. If test taking anxiety is severe, practise relaxation exercises.

OVERVIEW OF MEMORY TRAINING STEPS
- Spread your memory work over several sessions
- Recite material aloud
- Expect to remember (assume a positive attitude)
- Organise your material into a meaningful pattern
- Test and retest yourself
- Overlearn
- Use hooks, catchwords and silly sentences
- Study before sleeping.

Step 1. Spread out memory work

Sometimes students think that the longer they study, the more they will learn. Unfortunately, the reverse is true. Shorter periods of memory work – not more than two hours each – are far superior to six hours of frantic cramming.

Remember!
Reviewing memory work within 24 hours of the first study session is the most effective way to master the material.

Step 2. Recite material aloud

When you are studying or memorising, recite the answers to your study questions aloud so that you can hear the answer. Don't simply recite the answer in your head! That's a beginning, but *only* a beginning.

Research studies show that answering questions aloud improves recall by at least 80 per cent!

Question yourself aloud and answer yourself aloud.

If you study in a group or with a friend, quizzing one another will improve recall. Although your memory may begin to fail on a test, the voice of the person you studied with will often come through loudly and clearly.

Use all your senses
The more senses you involve in the learning process, the longer you will remember.

See it   *Read* and *visualise the material.*

Say it   *Answer questions* aloud that you formulate from your class notes. Use the cues in the recall column of your textbook and your notes to help you ask yourself study questions.

Write it   *Write* answers to questions from your study notes. Outline major points from the text.

Repeat it   *Repeat* this entire process until you have mastered the material.

Step 3. Expect to remember

Make a *decision* to remember! As obvious as this seems, many students fail to realise the power of an intent to recall. Because you want to remember a favourite song, you can easily repeat the lyrics word for word. If you *want* to remember, you will.

Your attitude is the secret. Believe in yourself and in your ability to learn.

Step 4. Organise the material

People who recall long lists of numbers often can do so because they have found a *pattern or a relationship*.

Look at this string of numbers and take a moment to try to memorise the list.

  3   6   9   12   15   18   21   24

(a) What is the pattern in this string of numbers?
    Write your answer below.

_____

(b) Do you see a pattern to these numbers?

  6   13   19   24   28   31   33   34

(c) Create *categories* to *organise visualisations* or *maps* of the information.

If you were trying to remember the names of students in one of your classes, how would you organise the material? Write your answer below.

_____

_____

(Turn page upside down for answers.)

(a) Increasing by 3 each time.
(b) Increasing by 7, by 6, by 5, etc. in a regular sequence each time.
(c) Perhaps you would use the same technique teachers use: they make seating charts and remember students by rows and specific seat location.

43

Step 5. Test and retest yourself

If you had to learn 10 definitions for class tomorrow, how could you test yourself? Would you write the definitions over and over or read the list aloud 20 times? Neither method is the best choice.

Instead, follow this self-testing process:

1. Memorise the first item.
2. Go on to the second item and memorise it.
3. Now repeat the first item and the second from memory.
4. When you know those two, go to the third.
5. Memorise the third item and repeat items one, two, and three.
6. Continue in this manner until all 10 definitions have been learned.

DON'T FORGET TO USE ALL YOUR SENSES

READ IT!   WRITE IT!   SAY IT!
SING IT!   IMAGINE IT!

Step 6. Overlearn

Revise material that you have learned several times. When final examinations or half-term come round, you will have mastered material that you have encoded for long-term recall. In maths classes, rework the model or sample five or more times to encode the correct process deeply.

- Commercials can haunt you for years because of the *constant repetition* of a jingle or song.

Step 7. Recall: use hooks, catchwords and silly sentences

Hooks

You hook the idea into your memory bank by using a *single letter* or *catchword* to pull up more information.

Most people have been taught ROY G BIV to remember the colours of the rainbow.

Red	Orange	Yellow
	Green	
Blue	Indigo	Violet

Catchwords

To remember these eight memory techniques, you can employ a similar hooking device.

S   Spread out memory work
R   Recite aloud
E   Expect to remember
O   Organise the material
T   Test and retest
O   Overlearn
R   Recall with hooks and catchwords etc
S   Study before sleeping

If the order is not important, you can create a catchword or phrase from the *first letter* of the words. The strange or bizarre is usually easier to remember.

You try it! Create a word by scrambling the above letters from the list of memory techniques. Spend no more than 5 minutes thinking.

(See author's suggested answer on page 46.)

Silly sentences

If words must be remembered in a specific order, then a *rhyming nonsensical* sentence may help you. In fact, the sillier the word or sentence, the easier it is to recall. For example, the colours of the rainbow mentioned under 'hooks' could be learned by a 'silly sentence' such as: **R**ead **O**ver **Y**our **G**reek **B**ook **I**n **V**acation (**R**ed, **O**range, **Y**ellow, **G**reen, **B**lue, **I**ndigo, **V**iolet.)

Step 8. Study before sleeping and upon awakening

To get the most mileage from study and memory work, *you should revise just before going to sleep*. Turn off the television and do not become otherwise distracted.

You will process this new material while you are sleeping. As you wake, revise again. To put a tight cap on the bottle of information you are encoding for future recall, *revise again* the same morning.

The author's suggested answer is the catchword ROOSTERS. Each letter is a signal for the first word of one of the eight memory techniques. If you want to remember even longer, *visualise* in your 'mind's eye' or associate the catchword with an object or a place with which you are already familiar. Can you remember the image of roosters in a picture book from your childhood, or even better, actual roosters that you have seen?

Visualise

Can you remember what ROOSTERS stands for?

R _____

O _____

O _____

S _____

T _____

E _____

R _____

S _____

Visualise for success

When you can visualise items from your text or classroom notes, they are much easier to recall. The rooster visualisation was an example of how to use association to remember. Simpler visual patterns can be just as effective. Whenever possible use 'mind maps' similar to the examples shown below to organise material (or create your own patterns). Once you've decided what information should be placed on your design, draw a new one and fill in the blanks from your memory.

Sample patterns

<u>Chronological time lines</u> for History classes

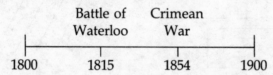

	Battle of Waterloo	Crimean War	
1800	1815	1854	1900

<u>Trees</u> are popular among biology students and genealogists, but can be used for many academic subjects.

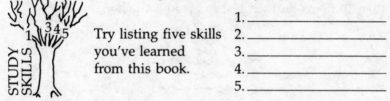

Try listing five skills you've learned from this book.

1. _____
2. _____
3. _____
4. _____
5. _____

Fill in this tree map using the five Rs on page 64.

<u>Flow chart</u>

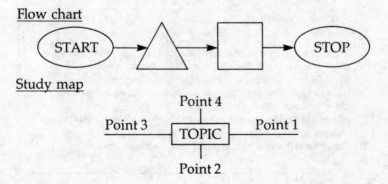

START → △ → □ → STOP

<u>Study map</u>

Point 4
Point 3 — TOPIC — Point 1
Point 2

<u>Sun shapes or clocks</u> for items that occur in a particular sequence

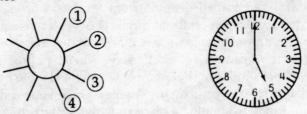

<u>Clustering</u> for short essays or branching lines

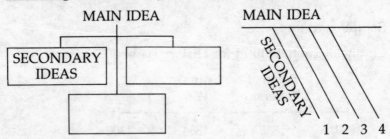

<u>Hand prints</u> – Ideas of equal importance. Speeches can also be given with greater ease using the hand print. Do not use more than 10 items on each test to avoid confusion.

Learning Trampolines

1. Map a chapter from a text or from a lecture in one of your classes using one or more of these techniques. Colour will also create a stronger glue for your mind and is highly recommended by cognitive psychologists. Try it several times before giving up on the technique.
2. Pick one of the visual patterns to map 12 techniques covered in this section.
3. Consolidate the information on SQ3R using a hand print.

Review of memory techniques

A.   The eight memory strategies

1. Spread memory work over several sessions

2. Recite material aloud

3. Expect to remember – assume a positive attitude

4. Organise material to be memorised into a logical pattern

5. Test and retest regularly

6. Overlearn

7. Use hooks, catchwords and silly sentences

8. Do memory work before sleeping

B.   Visualise for success

1. Use chronological time lines to remember dates

2. Sketch trees and fill in the branches with material to be learned

3. Use flow charts to remember things in sequence

4. Create a study map

5. Make sun shapes or clocks to remember the relation on various items

6. Cluster thoughts in an outline format

7. When there are ten or fewer items to learn, use hand prints

C.   Review this section of study skills strategies often

6. Exam Strategies

Lynne was a typical student who faced a common challenge – three major tests and a final examination would account for 60 per cent of her final grade. Often Lynne 'blanked out' in exams and found it difficult to finish during the time allotted. If you have felt this test-taking anxiety, you are not alone.

Successful students, however, have learned some sound strategies for test taking. If you understand the chapters presented earlier in this book on taking class notes, reading your textbook, and memory training, you are now ready to 'score' by learning test-taking strategies.

No test-taking secret or gimmick can be a substitute for thorough preparation!

Tips for taking objective tests

To do well on an objective test, you need to memorise facts and thoroughly understand concepts and relationships. The following hints should help you to score higher on true-false, matching, and fill-in-the-blank type questions. Ask your tutor what type of questions will be in the test, and then prepare accordingly.

Some hints:
- *Look over the entire test.* Know how much each question is worth and budget your time accordingly. Check the clock

every 10 minutes to ensure you will not be caught off guard and run out of time. If necessary, put your watch on the desk in front of you.

- *Answer the easiest questions first.* Tick those that are harder and return to those questions last. Otherwise, you will waste valuable time and miss answering the easier questions. Place another line through the tick when you complete the harder questions.
- *Underline key words in the question.* Make special note of negative words such as 'not'. Feel free, however, to ask your tutor for clarification if the question is vague or unclear.

True-false questions
- Answers containing such words as *'all'*, *'never'*, *'always'*, and *'everyone'* are usually wrong.
- On the other hand, qualifiers such as *'frequently'*, *'probably'*, and *'generally'* more often indicate a true answer.

Example

T   F   Class notes should *always* be rewritten.

The word 'always' is a clue that the answer may be false.

Multiple choice questions

1. *Draw a line through each answer which you eliminate.* (See example under 5 below.)

2. *Ensure that the grammatical structure* of the question agrees with your choice.

3. *Read all choices.* Even if the first answer seems correct, another choice may be better, or 'all of the above' may be the correct response.

4. *If you are at a complete loss, and there is no penalty for guessing, choose the longest answer* – especially on teacher-made exams.

5. *When opposite statements appear in a question, one of the statements is often correct.*

Example

When two opposite statements appear in a multiple choice question

    (a) one of the opposite statements is usually correct.
    (b) ~~neither is correct.~~
    (c) ~~both are correct.~~
    (d) ~~choice in the middle is often correct.~~

Matching questions

Approach matching question testing as a game and play by the rules.

Rule 1   As always, you begin by reading the question and underlining or numbering key words.

Rule 2   Glance over both columns quickly. Which column has the longer entries? Begin looking at that side so you can save time as you scan the shorter column for an answer each time.

Rule 3   Warning! Do not select an answer unless you are certain you've selected a correct match. Why? Because you've substantially reduced the number of items left for the more difficult final matches.

Rule 4   Circle or draw a line through each answer that you eliminate.

Rule 5   The game is coming to an end and now you will use your best guesstimate for the correct answer. Go ahead and guess at this point.

Essay examinations

Preparation for essay exams

Do essay exams create more anxiety for you than objective exams? Fear of unknown essay questions can be substantially reduced if you follow these three simple steps:

Step 1.   *Develop your own practice essay questions* by looking over your lecture notes and textbook assignments, and guessing what the instructor would select.

Step 2. *Sketch out a variety of outline responses* to 10 or more possible questions.

Step 3. *Memorise the outlines* using catch phrases or mnemonic (memory) devices.

Step 4. *Practise writing an essay* within a specific time constraint. This is especially helpful if you have difficulty completing your tests within the prescribed time.

Once you have revised and prepared for the test, you need to learn a few more skills that are particularly important on essay exams.

Essay writing skills

Skill 1. *Read each question carefully and underline key words in the different parts of the question.* When you are asked to 'trace' the development of social reform in Britain, you need to describe the historical development of the subject. On the other hand, when you are asked to 'criticise' a poem or book, your tutor expects you to show the positive and negative points and support your ideas with evidence.

Check your knowledge of direction words by filling in the blanks (answers at bottom of page)

1. *Compare* means to show the _____ between something and *contrast* requires that you explain the _____ between things.
2. *Justify* means to give _____ the for your ideas.
3. *Enumerate* simply means to _____ the main events or reasons.
4. *Describe* imples giving a _____ description of an event etc.

---

1. similarities, differences   2. reasons   3. list   4. detailed

5. *Evaluate* requires that you give the (a) _____ and negative points and your own (b) _____ on the issue.

Other words you will need to understand include:

evaluate	prove	illustrate
analyse	relate	diagram
delineate	state	discuss

If any are unfamiliar, look up their meaning in a dictionary.

Skill 2. Take a few minutes to analyse the entire test, and budget your time accordingly. Jot down the time available in the margin of the test.

Skill 3. Before writing, create an informal outline of the main ideas and supporting detail. Some students use a cluster outline similar to the one illustrated.

CLUSTER OUTLINE

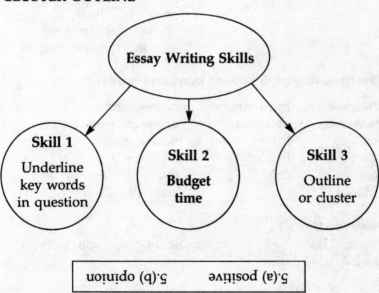

5.(a) positive   5.(b) opinion

Skill 4. Strive for a well-organised, focused essay. The most common complaint from teachers is that essays they read are too general and do not provide adequate support for the ideas presented. Avoid this problem by following the next three tips:

Common error	How to correct it
1. Padding	State your main point and stick to it. Avoid all extraneous material.
2. Weak development	Develop three main points. Provide details, examples and/or statistics.
3. Choppiness	Use transition words similar to those shown below to ensure that your essay is more coherent. Transition words will show relationships between sentences and paragraphs.

Practise using the following transition words!

therefore	furthermore	consequently
moreover	of course	on the other hand
first	in conclusion	nevertheless
since	in addition	admittedly
also	finally	thus
first of all	next	assuredly

Now you try it!
Practise clustering by referring to Skill 4. Check your work on the following page.

Essay question
Describe three common errors found in students' writing and *explain how to correct* those mistakes.

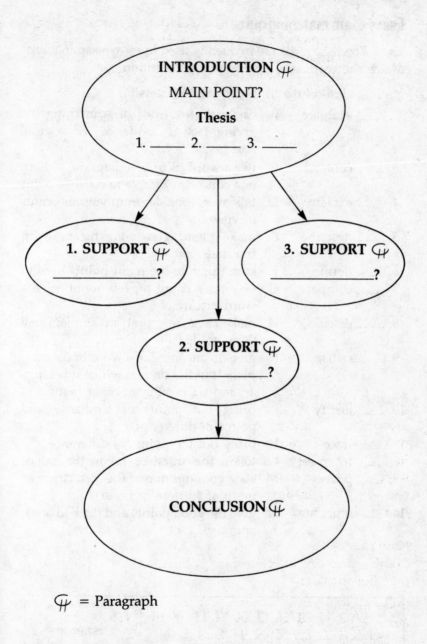

INTRODUCTION 𝒢

MAIN POINT?

Thesis

1. _____ 2. _____ 3. _____

1. SUPPORT 𝒢

_____?

3. SUPPORT 𝒢

_____?

2. SUPPORT 𝒢

_____?

CONCLUSION 𝒢

𝒢 = Paragraph

(Check your answer with that of the author on page 59.)

Essay exam matching quiz

The following words are frequently used in essay examinations. Match the word to the appropriate definition.

1. ___ summarise
2. ___ evaluate
3. ___ contrast
4. ___ explain
5. ___ describe
6. ___ define
7. ___ compare
8. ___ discuss
9. ___ critise
10. ___ justify
11. ___ trace
12. ___ interpret
13. ___ prove
14. ___ illustrate

A. show good reasons for

B. establish the truth of something by giving factual evidence or logical reasons

C. use a word picture, a diagram, a chart, or a concrete example to clarify a point

D. talk over; consider from various points of view

E. make plain; give your meaning of; translate

F. sum up; give the main points briefly

G. give an account of; tell about; give a word picture of

H. make clear; interpret; make plain; tell 'how' to do

I. give the meaning of a word or concept; place it in the class to which it belongs an and set it off from other items

J. bring out points of similarity and points of difference

K. bring out the points of difference

L. follow the course of; follow the trail of

M. state your opinion of the correctness or merit of an item or issue

N. give the good points and the bad ones; appraise

Answers: 1. F; 2. N; 3. K; 4. H; 5. G; 6. I; 7. J; 8. D; 9. M; 10. A; 11. L; 12. E; 13. B; 14. C.

Check your progress

Essay question

Describe the three common errors found in students' writing and *exlain how to correct* those mistakes.

Author's answer

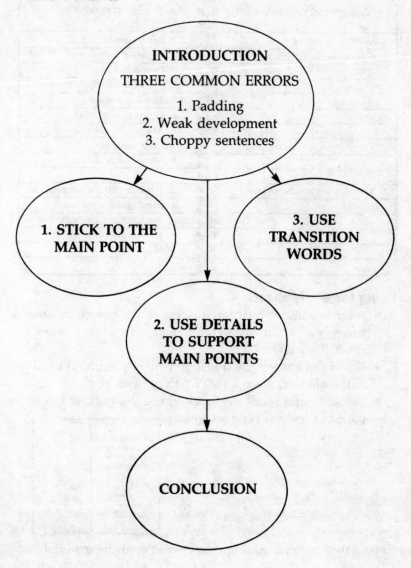

Other tips to prepare for exams

1. Use study sheets

A study sheet has the questions on one page, and the answers on another, as shown in the sample below.

QUESTIONS OR TERMS	TERMS
1. Explain 8 memory techniques (ROOSTERS)	1. Recite aloud.
	2. Organise the material.
	3. Overlearn.
	4. Spread out memory work.
	5. Test and retest.
	6. Expect to remember.
	7. Rely on the use of hooks, catchwords etc.
	8. Study before sleeping.
2. Why recite answers out loud?	2. If you can retrieve information (recall) you have excellent control over the material. Long-term memory is improved by 80 per cent.

Using the study sheets

- After writing or reciting answers to the questions several times, you are ready to *fold the page* as shown below to cover the answers.
- If you can answer the question correctly, without looking at the answer, place a (✔) by the question.
- If you cannot recall the answer, use the back of the paper to rewrite your response.

> 1. Explain 8 memory techniques (ROOSTERS)
>
> 2. Why recite answers out loud?

Repeat this process until you have mastered the material.

2. Use study cards

Some students use 3×5 index cards to help them study. Cards may be used for mathematics, science, English, history – almost any academic subject.

HAVE YOU USED FLASH CARDS?　　☐ YES　　☐ NO

(front)	WHAT IS THE ONLY WORD IN THE ENGLISH LANGUAGE THAT ENDS IN -SEDE?	SUPERSEDE	(back)
(front)	CIRCUMFERENCE = ?	πr^2	(back)
(front)	WHAT WORDS SUGGEST A FALSE ANSWER ON OBJECTIVE TESTS?	ALL, NEVER, ALWAYS	(back)

Step 1.　Look at the front side of the card and ask yourself the question.

Step 2.　Answer the question or define the concept. Then turn the card over to see if you are correct.

Step 3.　Correct? Place the card in a stack to your left.

Step 4.　Incorrect? Test and retest three times. Put that card in a stack to your right.

Step 5.　Have someone else ask you the questions repeating Steps 2 to 4.

Exam strategies review

Tick those you plan to practise.

For objective tests:

☐ Answer easiest questions first

☐ Underline key words in each question

☐ Cross out items you have answered

☐ Be alert for words such as 'always' and 'never'

☐ Ensure the grammatical structure of the answer is consistent with the question

☐ If there is no penalty for guessing, answer every question.

For essay exams:

☐ Anticipate questions the examiner might ask

☐ Sketch a variety of outline responses to model questions

☐ Practise writing sample essays

☐ Read each question carefully and underline key words

☐ Analyse the entire test before beginning to write

☐ Create an informal 'cluster' outline of your response before starting to write

☐ Strive for a focused essay, tightly organised and supported with facts.

7. Mathematics Study Skills

Mathematics requires special study skill techniques. This brief section will provide a few tips and ideas which should make your maths study skills more effective.

Because maths can be confusing, it will sometimes be necessary to ask for special help. If you become confused or lost, seek the assistance of your instructor or tutor. Mathematics often builds on a set of rules, and if basic principles are not understood, the likelihood is that you will stay lost.

Maths study skills tips

Tip 1 Copy all the theorems, principles, and definitions *exactly*. Do not paraphrase or condense anything that is written on the board. *Also* be sure to copy the tutor's explanation. Draw arrows to the explanation for each step of the problem.

Tip 2 Rewrite maths notes each day in ink for clarity and permanence. *Neatness* is especially important because of the need for accuracy.

Tip 3 *Rework model problems* over and over until you can do them without stopping. This is the crucial step that most students overlook. Instead of working out what is being taught in the model problem, they jump right into doing homework, and end up reworking problems several times.

Tip 4   Plan to work *at least two hours* on maths homework for every hour of class time. Since you may need to spend 10 to 12 hours working on maths class assignments, set your priorities carefully and take a lighter academic load if possible.

Tip 5   Learn the five Rs of maths shown below.

The five Rs of maths

- Recopy your notes
- Rework the model
- Recite out loud
- Recheck your work
- Test your answers for reasonableness.

Plan of attack

To help you to get an overview of the best maths study skills, read the following 5 Rs for maths and write marginal notations or recall cues to the left of R1, R2, R3, R4, and R5.

Recall cues

_____ **R1.** *Recopy your notes* in pen. Colour code definitions, rules and problem areas discussed by your tutor. Neatness and legibility are your first step towards becoming a better maths student.

How do you rate your maths notes?

☐ Organised and clear
☐ Messy
☐ Disorganised but neat.

_____ **R2.** *Rework the model* or example over and over until it can be done without hesitation.

Have you ever taken this step before beginning your homework?

☐ Yes ☐ No

If not, try it for a week and see if it makes a difference.

_____ **R3.** *Recite.* Oral recitation is one more technique for
_____ improving your mathematical skills. Practise this
_____ step with a study partner or friend. Force each
_____ other to explain aloud each step of the process. In
_____ case you are studying alone, still express your
thinking aloud.

Have you ever used this oral recitation technique when you were studying maths?

☐ Yes ☐ No

(Problem solving out loud is no longer the sign of
senility but the mark of a critical thinker.)

_____ **R4.** *Recheck* your computations. Also recheck your
_____ thinking process. This is even more important
_____ when you move from one step of a problem to the
next, or one concept to a new one.

*Mind chatter**

When the internal thinking of professionals was
questioned and recorded by Dr Arthur Whimbey
and Dr Jack Lochhead, a typical dialogue was
similar to the following:

1. 'Let me read the question again to be sure
   what's being asked. I'll circle or underline the
   question.'
2. 'Right, I see, but I'll read it again to be sure.'
3. 'Slow down. Don't rush.'
4. 'What is given? What is known?'
5. 'How can I use a diagram, make a chart, or draw
   a diagram to help me?'

In all cases, lawyers, doctors, engineers etc were
painstakingly careful to reread phrases and double
check their work.

* Adapted from *Problem Solving and Comprehension*, Whimbey and Lochhead,
Lawrence Erlbaum Associates, 1986.

_____**R5.** *Test for reasonableness.* Plug your answer into the problem to see if it makes sense. This final check could save you both time and embarrassment later.

Asking questions about how reasonable an answer is will make critical thinking a habit and problem solving less ominous.

Maths strategies review

Maths study skill tips

- Copy all theorems, principles and definitions carefully and exactly

- Rewrite maths notes in ink – be neat

- Rework model problems until they become second nature

- Spend two hours of homework for each hour of class time.

The five Rs of maths

- R1 Recopy your work

- R2 Rework model problems

- R3 Recite aloud to explain each step of the problem-solving process

- R4 Recheck your work

- R5 Test for reasonableness – ensure that your answer makes sense.

If you are confused, do not wait to get help. The longer you are lost, the more likely you'll stay lost!

8. Final Coaching Review

You have now completed this short intensive study skills programme. Your score in the review quiz on the next page will indicate the progress you have made in a very short time.

How can you continue to make progress? How can you learn to be a skilful student as well as a critical thinker? How can you use this information to improve your performance?

Follow the plan below and apply your skills.

Action: rerun the bases

Day 1   *Discipline your time!* Make a revised timetable using the blank on page 23. Place this timetable in your notebook and above your desk. Use it for two or three weeks, but modify as necessary. You are in charge of all changes, and should allow yourself *some* flexibility.

Day 2   Take class notes using the model format on page 28. Create study questions and highlight your notes today. Revise for 5–10 minutes as soon after each class as possible. Also, revise all the abbreviations and begin using them.

Day 3   *Don't stop now!* Return to the reading skills section on page 33. Apply the SQ3R techniques to this book. Mark your own copy of this book as you would any other text.

Day 4   *Be persistent!* Apply your study skills to a magazine article, or any other material you want to study critically.

Day 5   Take 30 minutes to revise the entire memory section and memorise the concepts of learning indicated by the catchword ROOSTERS. Use this principle for one of your classes.

Day 6   Take 30 minutes to memorise the hints for taking objective examinations. *You can do it!* Create a catchword or silly sentence of your own. Remember to recite aloud or study with another person.

Day 7   You are now an excellent candidate for success because you are applying a plan of action that can become a pattern of learning for a lifetime.

Final review quiz

Choose the best possible multiple choice, fill in the blank, or true/false answer.

_____   1.   Notes should be revised within
(a) 72 hours
(b) 24 hours
(c) 48 hours
(d) none of the above

_____   2.   When two opposite statements appear in a multiple choice question
(a) one of the opposite statements is usually correct
(b) neither is correct
(c) both are correct
(d) choice in the middle is often correct.

_____   3.   Recall cues are placed in the _____ margin of the paper.

_____   4.   Reciting answers to study questions improves memory by
(a) 82 per cent
(b) 95 per cent
(c) 70 per cent
(d) none of the above.

T   F   5.   Study time should be divided into blocks of three to four hours.

T   F   6.   All notes should be rewritten or typed except for maths notes.

T   F   7.   Visual organisers are best suited to art classes.

T   F   8.   'Mind chatter' is 'internal dialogue' used by professional problem solvers to find solutions.

T   F   9.   Read through a paragraph before you underline or highlight.

T   F   10. SQ3R is a reading strategy developed for surveying and skimming easy material.

Check answers below.

Place your score in here ☐

Each question is worth 10 points, so if you miss two you earned 80/100 or 80 per cent. If you scored less than 70 per cent, revise the appropriate section of this book with more focused attention.

Answers to final review

Hint. Save all old tests for revision for half terms and final examinations.

Check your progress. Read carefully the explanation on questions that you missed.

Question	Answer	Explanation
1.	B	Revise class notes as soon as possible, certainly within 24 hours so that abbreviations and garbled notes can be clarified.
2.	A	Often one of two opposite statements is correct in a multiple choice question.

3.   Left   Recall cues are placed on the left side on the margin.

4.   D   'None of the above' was correct; 80 per cent is the actual answer.

5.   F   Study time is best broken into 1 and 1½ hour intervals with ten minute breaks.

6.   F   Instead of recopying notes, study time is better spent writing study questions, recall phrases, and reciting answers out loud. Maths notes should, however, be recopied.

7.   F   Visual organisers like trees, maps etc can be used in any subject.

8.   T   Professional problem solvers think methodically and 'talk' themselves through the problem.

9.   T   To avoid too much underlining, read a paragraph first and then underline the important points when you reread it.

10.   F   SQ3R is used when reading difficult or complex material.

Further Reading from Kogan Page

How to Study: A Student's Guide to Effective Learning Skills, Anne Howe

How to Succeed in A Levels, 2nd edition, Howard Barlow

Learning to Teach Practical Skills: A Self-Instruction Guide, Ian Winfield

Staying the Course: How to Survive Higher Education, edited by John Gilbert

Where to Study in the UK: A Guide to British Professional Qualifications